goat
kid

duck
duckling

cat
kitten

elephant
calf

Like you, they love to play.

gorilla
infant

dog
puppy

They love to eat.

monkey
infant

chipmunk
pup

koala
joey

turtle
hatchling

They love to
make noise.

bird
chick

hippopotamus
calf

SPLASH

They love to snuggle.

bear
cub

rabbit
kitten